learn to
Relax

how to feel calmer
and more in control
of your life

Nicola Jenkins

This is a Parragon Book
First published in 2003

PARRAGON
Queen Street House
4 Queen Street
Bath BA1 1HE, UK

Produced by
THE BRIDGEWATER BOOK COMPANY LTD

Photography by
MIKE HEMSLEY AT WALTER GARDINER PHOTOGRAPHY

Photographic models:
ADAM CARNE, ANNE POWER

Hardback ISBN: 1-40542-296-3
Paperback ISBN 1-40542-298-X

Printed in China

The views expressed in this book are those of the author
but they are general views only. Any reader taking
prescription medication or who is pregnant must be
especially careful to consult a doctor before using any part
of the remedies described in this book. Parragon hereby
exclude all liability to the extent permitted by law for any
errors or omissions in this book and for any loss, damage or
expense (whether direct or indirect) suffered by a third
party relying on any information contained in this book.

contents

what happens to the body under stress

Λ Stress release
Experts say that placing your head in your hands like this can help you find creative ways around a problem.

Recent statistics suggest that as much as 70 per cent of all visits to doctors involve conditions that are stress-related or that are made worse by stress. Stress is literally making us sick. If you are reading this book, then it is likely that you are already aware of some of the effects of stress on your own life or on the lives of those closest to you. You may be facing a serious physical disorder, recovering from a heart condition, having problems sleeping, or dealing with a range of emotional symptoms that are seriously affecting your ability to enjoy life.

A little bit of stress can be good for you. It makes you feel alert, able to concentrate effectively and perform to a high standard. With this, you often get a sense of euphoria, a natural high that arises because you have been able to meet a challenge successfully. That feeling of euphoria is addictive, however, which is why you may be tempted to continue at the pace you have set yourself, and why it can be a surprise when, after some time of performing at that level, your body begins to slow down and unpleasant side effects emerge.

Recognising that a problem exists is half the battle; the other half is committing to making changes in the way you do things so that you are able to relax. Commitment to relaxation means making changes, even if it involves letting go of long-standing habits, and keeping to the new habits once you have found what works for you. It is very easy to slip back into old habits when you are no longer focussing on your needs.

The following pages offer a range of simple, effective techniques that can help you to adjust your response to stress and aid relaxation. Before you try each and every suggestion, remember that you and your circumstances are special and unique – taking up a creative and expensive hobby isn't going to help you relax if the main reason you are under stress is because of severe financial burdens. Several small steps that can be integrated into your existing life are more likely to be effective, and will be easier to stick to.

In the 1920s, Dr Hans Seyle first described what has become known as the general adaptive response to stress. Seyle argued that there were three stages to stress:

∧ *Effects of stress*
Too much stress can cause physical, emotional and behavioural problems.

Stage 1 Alarm

This is the body's initial response to stress. During this stage, the body responds by initiating 'fight-or-flight' mechanisms.

Nerves send messages to the adrenal glands, telling them to release more adrenaline so that you are able to respond quickly. The immediate effect is that your blood volume and blood pressure rise, so that your heart, brain and skeletal muscles get the nutrients and oxygen they need. Your heart beats faster to keep the blood flowing to these critical organs, and blood-sugar levels increase so that you have the energy to fight or run away from whatever is causing the stress. The branching vessels in your lungs, the bronchioles, also dilate, allowing more air to enter the lungs, so that more oxygen becomes available to the body. Blood vessels in other areas of the body constrict to limit the supply of blood to parts not required for immediate survival.

Stage 2 Resistance

During the Resistance stage, the stressor has been around for some time and the body is adapting to its continuing presence. Long-term changes start to occur in the body to deal with the load added by the stressor. Instead of responding to stress by sending messages via the nervous system to the adrenal glands to release adrenaline, your body adapts to the long-term presence of the stressor by changing the levels of hormones in the body. This enables a slower, more easily controlled response.

Emotionally, you may have adapted somewhat to the new stressor, and it no longer produces the same level of response from you. You may have integrated any changes into your life to a certain degree, and feel that you are coping reasonably well. There may be certain physical symptoms developing to indicate that you aren't at your best; possibly you are aware of being frequently tired, or suffering from a range of other symptoms that appear mild when examined separately.

Stage 3 Exhaustion

At the Exhaustion stage, the body recognises that it is no longer able to cope with the continuing demands placed on it by the stressor or by a number of stressors. Resistance to stress and disease is severely reduced. Heart attacks and severe, debilitating infections are more likely. Cortisol and other adrenal hormones have been present at high levels within the body for a long time. If cortisol levels remain high for extended periods, then any stored proteins within the body can be broken down, blood pressure will rise and more long-term changes can occur. This includes slower healing of cartilage and bone, loss of muscle tone, loss of bone protein and a lowered immune response.

At this stage, you may be experiencing more severe symptoms, telling you it is time to take action to reduce stress.

Cortisol

The key hormone involved in helping the body to adapt to long-term stress is cortisol. Normally it helps to keep your blood-sugar levels stable between meals and to maintain the volume of water in the blood vessels. However, when you are under a great deal of stress, you start to produce more cortisol. At high levels, cortisol will start to make sugar out of other substances – such as fat or protein, so that these can be used to provide alternative sources of energy for the body. This has a knock-on effect on other hormones with the result that you start to retain more water. For this reason some people experience bloating when under stress.

∧ Fight-or-flight
Raised adrenaline levels that prepare you to fight or run can increase aggression but also produce a sense of euphoria.

◁ Tend-or-befriend
Seeking out supportive friends or becoming more nurturing can be effective ways of combating stress.

Tend-or-befriend: Another kind of stress response

Recent research carried out by Dr Shelley Taylor, a psychologist at the University of California, Los Angeles, suggests that there is also another model for the way people adapt to stress. Dr Taylor refers to this as the 'tend-or-befriend' model, which appears to be more common in females than males. It refers to the tendency in humans (and other mammals) for females, when under stress, to nurture themselves and their young and to form strong alliances within a larger group.

This model does not exclude or replace the fight-or-flight instinct; Dr Taylor argues that it is probably just as long-standing: when humans still lived in caves, a female's aggression would have been more likely to be limited to the defence of herself and her children.

This response is due to the release of oxytocin – a hormone that enhances relaxation, reduces fear and promotes nurturing. When under stress, this hormone would help to ensure that a woman did not run away, but stayed to protect any children.

The tend-or-befriend model provides a biological reason why women in particular prefer to be with others, especially other women, when they are under stress, and why women are more likely to seek out social support mechanisms than men. We can learn from this that seeking nurture and support are effective aids to reducing stress, whether you are male or female.

signs and symptoms of stress

Each one of us experiences stress in a completely personal way and exhibits the symptoms of stress in a unique fashion. No matter how stressed you are, it is highly unlikely that you will be showing all the physical, emotional and behavioural symptoms of stress. Instead you will show patterns of symptoms that vary according to how badly stressed you are. Learning to recognise your personal early signs of stress, and taking effective steps to relax at that point, can head off the more severe symptoms you might face later on.

∧ Exercise
Taking regular exercise is a great way of calming the mind, which is a key step in learning to relax.

PHYSICAL SYMPTOMS

Increased alertness (initially)

Increased heart rate

Increased blood pressure

Muscle tension (especially in the upper back, neck, chest and jaw)

Increased headaches and migraines

Suppressed immune system

Raised blood-sugar levels

Increased metabolic rate

Lowered blood supply to extremities, so poor circulation gets worse

Lowered blood supply to skin means increased likelihood of skin complaints

Lowered absorption of nutrients in bowel

Less movement in digestive system means increased risk of constipation and IBS symptoms

Bowel disorders increase, including diarrhoea, constipation, nausea, vomiting and ulcers

Kidneys retain sodium and water, higher risk of oedema and bloating

Disturbed sleep or insomnia

Breathing becomes faster and more shallow

Dry mouth

Lowered resistance to viruses (such as the common cold, cold sores or similar)

Lowered libido or impotence

Lowered sperm count

Menstrual cycle disrupted

Fertility decreased in both men and women

∨ Double trouble
Stress can make you withdraw from others and stop you wanting to communicate with loved ones.

EMOTIONAL SYMPTOMS

Increased irritability

Increased anger or hostility

Depression

Jealousy

Restlessness

Anxiety

Inability to make decisions

Withdrawing from others

Avoiding social events

Lack of interest in others

Tearfulness

Over-critical of self or others

Tendency to put oneself down

Inability to see positive aspects of one's situation

Obsessive focus on an event, situation or person, unable to be distracted from the problem area

>Signs of stress
Signs that you are under too much stress range from restlessness and anxiety to sexual disinterest and comfort eating.

∨ Bottling it up
A popular source of comfort, alcohol actually increases the physical stress on your body and could send physical symptoms spiralling out of control.

BEHAVIOURAL SYMPTOMS

Increased smoking

Increased alcohol use

Increased use of recreational drugs

Over-eating or comfort-eating

Under-eating or skipping meals (loss of appetite)

Changed eating habits (or tastes in food)

Lethargy

Becoming more accident-prone

Compulsive behavioural patterns (such as a sudden urge to wash hands, etc)

Sexual disinterest

Speech difficulties, including stuttering, stammering

Displacement activities to avoid urgent tasks, for instance, excessive television viewing

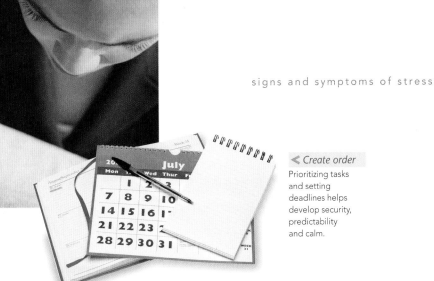

◄ Create order
Prioritizing tasks
and setting
deadlines helps
develop security,
predictability
and calm.

Severe Stress

You are more likely to experience severe side effects of stress if you:

Set yourself extremely high standards

Find it difficult to say 'no'

Feel you are constantly in danger of letting yourself or others down

Lose sight of the difference between minor and major problems and overreact to minor ones

Become unable to prioritize between minor and major or urgent and non-urgent tasks

Avoid the major or urgent tasks, spending too much time on less demanding activities

Get impatient when things don't happen when you want them to

Insist that the way you do things is the right or best way

Feel guilty that you 'should' or 'ought' to be doing more

Are unable or unwilling to delegate tasks or ask for help

Regularly double-book yourself for events etc.

Taking action to combat stress

Research into people's physical and emotional responses to stress has led the experts to agree that stressors that are unpredictable and uncontrollable have a significantly worse effect on the individual than those situations where they can exert some control. Repeated exposure to these unexpected events leads to long-term debilitating effects, including severe depression. To promote relaxation, you need to do the following:

REDUCE STRESS. Avoid the source, or take significant action to change how it affects you.

CHANGE YOUR REACTION TO STRESS. Develop coping strategies to deal with stress.

FIND AN OUTLET FOR FRUSTRATION. Don't bottle it up, but find a harmless way of releasing your tension.

ENHANCE YOUR PERSONAL SENSE OF CONTROL. Develop security or predictability in other aspects of your life.

ten steps
to relaxation

The following steps can help you to reduce stress, change your response to it or regain a sense of control in your life. Finding effective outlets for your frustration needs consideration. Take time to think about activities that excite or inspire you. The outlet you choose needs to be something that you are going to really enjoy; finding time to relax is difficult enough without using that time to punish yourself.

∧ *Healing touch*
A shoulder and neck massage can help to reduce some of the physical symptoms of stress.

1 Catch your breath

Monitoring your breathing is one of the easiest and most effective ways to achieve a deep sense of relaxation. When you are under stress, it is common to start to take faster and more shallow breaths. To relax, you need to reverse the process:

BREATHE FROM YOUR DIAPHRAGM. This allows your lungs to fully inflate, which means you will get more oxygen to your brain and body whilst calming the mind. If you are breathing from your diaphragm, your abdomen will also move as you inhale and exhale. Try breathing in this fashion for ten slow inhalations, pausing before slowly exhaling. At the end of this time, you should feel very relaxed, if not euphoric.

Burn frankincense

This essential oil actively encourages you to breathe more deeply, as well as opening the airways in the lungs. Used for centuries in churches, it helps to create a meditative atmosphere and aids deep breathing and a calm approach to crises.

COUNT TO TEN. This old favourite really works, allowing you time to calm down before responding in times of crisis. Rather than over-reacting to a new stressor, sit down, count to ten slowly, taking a few deep breaths, then proceed, only moving slower than you did before.

DON'T RUSH. Make every effort to give yourself enough time to complete your tasks and get to where you need to be without becoming panicked. Soothing music played en route will also help you to relax.

USE PUBLIC TRANSPORT. If the transport infrastructure is suitable for your journey you have a chance to sit down on the train or bus. Then you can catch up on tasks whilst travelling or relax with a book or gentle music.

◁ *Breathe!*
Essential oils that encourage deep, relaxed breathing include frankincense, cedarwood, lavender, sandalwood, rosewood, marjoram and benzoin.

2 Create a haven

A haven can be found or built anywhere. It should be a space where you feel totally comfortable and secure, where you can control the sights, sounds and textures, and where you also have some control over who attracts your attention. In your haven you can relax and recuperate from the daily grind.

SELECT CALM COLOURS. Generally, lighter, softer colours and pastels are deemed to be more relaxing than strong, vibrant colours. Soft mauves, pinks, blues and greens all help to calm the mind, relax the body and reduce anger or frustration. Strong yellows, oranges and reds tend to stimulate the body and mind, and should be avoided in large amounts in areas where you seek relaxation.

USE SOUND TO CHANGE THE ATMOSPHERE. Tibetan chimes, Balinese bells, singing bowls and similar space-cleansing agents are excellent for altering the atmosphere of your room. If your haven doubles as your living room, use these when you first enter the home at the end of the day, or if people have been arguing.

ADD PLANTS OR OTHER ASPECTS OF NATURE. As well as bringing harmony to your surroundings by adding the colour green, plants take in carbon dioxide and release oxygen during respiration. Increased oxygen helps you to think more clearly.

Colours for calmness

If you are already experiencing high blood pressure, reducing the amounts of stronger colours in areas of your life outside the home can also have a beneficial effect. Why not replace red folders and desk equipment with blue ones?

Reduce noise levels

Try working in a quiet room, lowering the ringer tone on the telephone, or screening calls for part of the day. If you work in an open-plan environment or are hot desking, try using a personal stereo or earplugs to reduce the effect of stressful distractions. At home, try muting the television, telephone and radio output. Invest in double glazing to cut out street noise. Alter the kind of music you listen to. Choose music that has a slow rhythm and makes you feel relaxed and uplifted.

Play classical music

Classical music, especially if it does not involve singing, has long been held to be calming. Recent reports indicate that Mozart's music in particular is very effective at reducing stress and anxiety, and aiding study.

GET A PET. Research indicates that time spent stroking or petting an animal helps to reduce blood pressure and heart rate.

CHANGE THE LIGHTING. Bright and overhead lights help to stimulate the mind and keep it alert. To aid relaxation, use low lighting in your haven. Put low-wattage bulbs in lamps, dim overhead lamps or light candles instead.

REDUCE OR GET RID OF CLUTTER. Remove any clutter from the space you have designated as your haven, or at least stack it neatly out of sight. If your clutter involves paperwork and similar activities, set aside time to deal with it.

USE COMFORTABLE FURNISHINGS. Any furnishings in your haven need to be completely relaxing. Change the decor if there is anything that you don't like or that upsets you.

GET AN IONIZER. These electrical appliances are now readily available and help to reduce the levels of chemical pollutants, pollen, dust and dirt to manageable levels within a room. People using ionizers often report improved sleep and a more relaxed state of mind.

AIR THE ROOM REGULARLY. Airing your haven helps to increase the amount of oxygen in the air. It removes stale odours and enhances the sense of calm and relaxation within.

USE FRAGRANCES. Air fresheners or essential oils in a vaporizer can add a calming touch to your haven. Use up to ten drops in a vaporizer for a lasting effect.

MAINTAIN THE ROOM TEMPERATURE. Your haven should be at a comfortable temperature. Whilst finances might suggest that you need to limit the amount of heating you use, remember that feeling cold for a long time increases stress and puts pressure on your immune system, making you more vulnerable to infections.

∧ *Your haven*
Create your own haven with calm colours, comfortable furnishings, peaceful sounds and elements from nature.

3 Make time to take time

The most common problem associated with being under stress is a lack of time to do what you want to do. Yet there are often small habits that we have that, when examined or altered, can save us the time we need in order to get some breathing space.

KEEP A DIARY FOR TWO WEEKS. Be as honest as you can be about everything you do. This will show when you are most and least effective. To make the diary even more insightful, give an indication as to how you felt at the time – stressed, relaxed, worried, happy, sad, etc.

HANDLE EACH PIECE OF PAPER ONLY ONCE. Unanswered letters and unpaid bills can easily mount up if they are allowed to. See how long it takes you to deal with a problem by making a pencil mark in one corner of the piece of paper each time you touch it. Rather than avoiding the paperwork, make the effort to handle each item only once, even if this means you leave all letters and bills to be dealt with once a week.

RATIONALISE YOUR SHOPPING. Frequent trips to the supermarket can be stressful and a waste of time. Try going less often but picking up everything you need for a week or two. Alternatively, order your groceries over the internet. Even if the supermarket charges a delivery fee, think of it as an investment in your sanity.

Make a list

Writing lists of things to do is extremely helpful if you worry that you might forget something important. You can also use these lists to help you to prioritize your tasks, so that the most important things get done first.

DELEGATE. There are usually many tasks in the home and workplace that may be open to delegation. Even if the person you delegate them to doesn't do the tasks the same way as you, allowing the individual to try helps develop his or her own skills and eases the pressure off you. If you are badly overworked and feel you have no one to support you at work, you may want to discuss this issue with your employer to see if any help is available.

USE AN ANSWERPHONE. Even if you are home, screen your telephone calls for at least part of the day, for instance during meal times, and save returning those calls for a time when you are able to concentrate on the person phoning.

REWARD YOURSELF. Draw up a list of things you would like to do if you had the time and treat yourself to one of them each time you tackle a major or urgent task you know you have been avoiding.

USE A DIARY OR CALENDAR. Get into the habit of recording all appointments or social events in one place. This will help you to co-ordinate any events with partners or other household members as well as ensuring that you don't double-book yourself. Remember to timetable in your relaxation rewards!

COMMIT TO YOURSELF. Once you have found the time and space in which to relax, don't let anyone else put anything in that time. You have worked for the time off, you have earned it, now you need to go and enjoy it! Do not allow yourself to feel guilty or to use this time to carry out a chore. Taking time off, even if it is only half an hour to have a soak in the bath, will leave you relaxed and refreshed and better able to cope with existing problems.

LIFE STAGE STRESSORS INCLUDE

Moving house

Change or loss of relationship

Parents' or children's change or loss of relationship

Redundancy or loss of job

Change of job

Financial concerns

Pregnancy

Physical illness

Examinations

Family members moving or leaving home

Change of sleeping habits

Bereavement

Personal injury

Bullying or harassment at work or school

▼ Shopping
Save time and effort by shopping online when it suits your schedule.

❯ On demand
Screening calls lets you control how and when you deal with telephone interruptions.

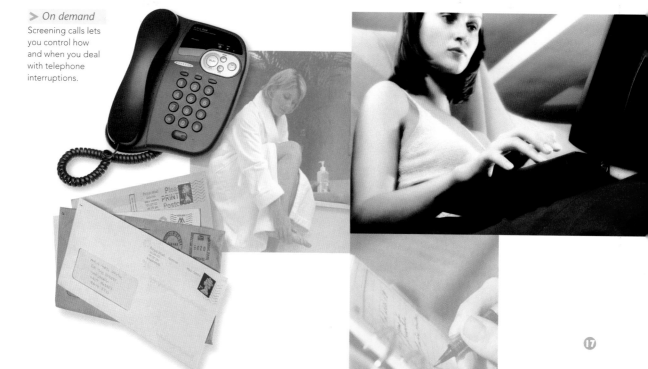

17

4 Calm the mind

Mental exercises, however simple, make the greatest difference in helping you to relax. Without calming the mind, physical relaxation is virtually impossible. Even if you keep meditations or visualization activities to five minutes a day, their effects are very long lasting.

MEDITATION. One of the most effective methods of relaxation, meditation helps you to focus and clear your mind, reducing the effect of whatever problems are worrying you. It also requires next to no equipment. To prepare for meditation, simply select a comfortable place to sit or lie down, where your back is straight and your limbs are arranged comfortably, and where you are not going to be disturbed by distractions or changes in temperature. Close your eyes and counting the inhalations focus on your breathing. Concentrate on slowing it down. Allow your mind to drift, even if it goes back to the problems that are worrying you. Don't worry if you find it difficult to meditate for more than five minutes at the start; this is normal. If you persevere you will soon see results.

WALKING MEDITATION. If you find it difficult to sit still to meditate, try a walking meditation. This can be done anywhere, either in your garden, in your home or out in nature. It is important that you walk slowly

Affirmations

These are short sentences that you repeat whenever positive thinking is required. As well as helping you to put a positive spin on any situation that is worrying you, these sentences can be used to help you to relax if you say them either out loud or to yourself every time you are thinking about an issue that worries you. Try 'Creative solutions and wonderful opportunities present themselves to me constantly', for example. Remember, the more you repeat them, the more effective they become.

through the area you have chosen, allowing your mind to clear. Watch the pace at which you walk; you are more likely to speed up when thinking of a problem. When this happens, stop, look around you and stand still until you are able to release the problem, then walk on, only more slowly.

CREATIVE VISUALIZATION. This can be done as part of a meditation, or at any other time. Think of it as daydreaming with a purpose. For this exercise you need to imagine yourself in a particularly calm and serene environment, either a place you know or somewhere you would like to be – a hammock on the beach, perhaps? Picture yourself there as clearly as you can. As you become more comfortable with the visualization process, you can introduce new elements to it; why not picture a waiter arriving at your hammock not only with a tropical drink, but also with something that represents a good working solution to whatever problem you are facing?

EMOTIONAL STRESS RELEASE. Kinesiologists refer to a particular area of your forehead as the emotional stress release point; this is where you place your hand automatically if you rest your head on it. Simply resting your head in this position for a few seconds can help to calm you down and is also a very effective way of encouraging you to think laterally – and find those creative solutions.

EXERCISE. Any form of physical activity can be a great way of calming the mind and providing a positive outlet for releasing any lingering frustration or rage. Choose an activity that you enjoy and that will take your mind off your worries. The most effective exercises for calming the mind are those that require you to concentrate on your breathing whilst working (such as swimming, long-distance running or yoga) or that are complex enough that you need to focus your mind on your actions whilst working (try any aerobics class or martial art, horse-riding, sailing or windsurfing). For best effects, pick an activity that takes place outside, as the fresh air can make a big difference.

⌄ *Walking tall*
Wherever you go, walk with your head up; you're guaranteed a better view and a sunnier disposition than if you focus only on your feet.

‹ *Visualization*
Concentrate on visualizing your personal version of serenity.

‹‹ *Focus*
Martial arts, such as Tai Chi or Chi Qong, can help you achieve clarity of mind.

19

5 Massage for partners

Massage is an extremely effective way of aiding relaxation as well as improving communication between partners if stress or conflicting demands have contributed to a loss of intimacy. If time allows, treat yourselves to a warm, relaxing bath before starting the massage. Not only will this enhance the effects of the massage, but it will also soften up the muscles a bit before you work on them, making the treatment more effective.

Don't be surprised if there is an urge to fall asleep after the treatment. This means you are doing a good job! Regular massage, even if it is only a ten-minute treatment three times a week, can make a huge difference to your approach to life and to each other. The following short treatment for the back concentrates on those areas prone to stress-related muscular aches and pains.

BACK MASSAGE. To encourage deep relaxation during the massage, make sure that your partner is lying comfortably, either on the floor or on the bed. In either case, you will need to kneel beside him or her to carry out the treatment.

Gently warm any oil or lotion that you will be using during the treatment before applying it – try putting the bottle of oil in a bowl of warm water beforehand.

< knuckling

∨ effleurage

< Massage oils
Roman or German chamomile are particularly good for muscle relaxation.

∧ kneading

EFFLEURAGE. Apply the oil in smooth, flowing strokes, working from the hips up to the shoulders and neck, then gliding down the sides of the body back to the hips to repeat. Keep this stroke rhythmic, slow and smooth. Repeat until you can feel the skin and muscles warming and relaxing beneath your hands. Repeat for smaller areas as well, concentrating on the hips and waist area, the mid-back and then the shoulders.

KNEADING TO THE BACK. This movement involves you picking up the flesh with one hand then passing it to the other in a side to side movement. Work your way up one side of the body then down the other, spending more time on the shoulders, where most people hold a lot of tension. Remember to keep the movements slow and rhythmic. The slower you go, the more relaxing the movement is for the person you are treating.

▼ *petrissage*

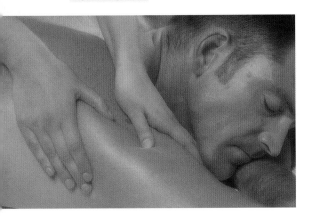

KNUCKLING. This uses the first joint of the fingers to work deeper into tight muscles and is particularly useful over the shoulders and hips. Place your knuckles on your partner's back, keeping your wrists straight (so that you can lean in with your body weight and press deeper), and rotate your hands from the wrists. This movement is very relaxing if done slowly and is also very effective if your partner has extremely tense muscles. It also saves your hands and wrists if you find the massage painful to perform.

PETRISSAGE. Use your thumbs to make small, grinding circles about the size of a ten-pence piece. This movement is great for releasing particularly tight muscles and feels wonderful when done very slowly. Use this movement around the shoulder blade and along the tight bands of muscle often found on either side of the spine. After you have tried the small circles and repeated the movement at least three times, press just as hard and run your thumbs along the area you have just worked on.

Knead the neck with one hand, then follow up with small petrissage movements just below the base of the skull.

Repeat the kneading and then the smooth flowing effleurage strokes. As you are about to finish the massage, gradually make your strokes slower and lighter until you are just stroking your partner very gently.

6 Try natural remedies for stress

Alternative therapies offer a huge range of treatments and remedies for stress and are generally extremely effective at aiding relaxation. Each person has a unique response to treatment, so finding the best method for you can be a great experiment. Speak to friends and relatives in the first instance; often they will be able to recommend a therapist. Most therapies also offer ways that can help you to relax in-between treatments, some of which are listed below:

FLOWER REMEDIES Bach Flower remedies are available in most health food shops and chemists and provide emotional support in times of trouble. To use them, you just take a few drops either in a glass of water or straight on to your tongue several times a day.

Try Centaury if you find you are taking on too much, Elm if you find responsibility overwhelming, Hornbeam if you are aware that you are delaying taking action, Impatiens if you are impatient or frustrated, Oak or Olive if you are exhausted and have to keep going. Don't forget the blended Rescue Remedy for severe shock, exam stress or mental anguish.

∧ *Homeopathy*
Most remedies work best if you avoid tea, coffee or strong peppermint sweets. Switch to non-minty flavours of toothpaste too.

Hand reflexology

Any form of reflexology is extremely good for reducing stress and aiding relaxation. Hand reflexology allows you to treat yourself at any time during the day, especially when you are feeling particularly stressed. The solar plexus point – in the centre of your palm, directly below your middle finger – is the place to work if you are feeling very upset. This is often sensitive to touch when you are very stressed. Rotate your thumb over the spot, pressing down in small circles. Press as hard as you can comfortably do.

HOMEOPATHY There is a wide variety of homeopathic remedies that ease some of the symptoms of stress. Gelsemium is useful if you feel anxious about forthcoming exams, interviews or presentations. Lachesis helps if you are suffering from mental or physical exhaustion as a result of working too hard. Lycopodium aids those experiencing a lack of self-confidence and mood swings. Nat. mur is useful for those feeling tearful or over-sensitive who also experience water retention and migraines as a result of stress. Staphysagria is useful when your response to stress includes feelings of resentment, anger or humiliation. If you want to find a blend that is carefully chosen to meet your personal needs, contact a professional homeopath.

> **Lavender**
Use lavender to make sedating sachets to fragrance bedlinens.

∨ **Flower remedies**
Take these in a glass of water or directly on the tongue.

∧ **Reflexology**
Work the solar plexus point in the centre of the palm to subtly reduce the effects of stress.

< **Blissful bathing**
Warm baths are more relaxing than hot ones. Add sea salt, sodium bicarbonate or essential oils to reduce anxiety.

ESSENTIAL OILS FOR RELAXATION AND TO REDUCE STRESS

Benzoin	Melissa
Bergamot	Neroli
Cedarwood	Orange
Clary Sage	Palmarosa
Coriander	Patchouli
Frankincense	Petitgrain
Geranium	Roman
German	chamomile
chamomile	Rose
Ginger	Rosewood
Grapefruit	Sandalwood
Jasmine	Tangerine
Lavender	Vetiver
Lemon	Yarrow
Marjoram	Ylang ylang
May chang	

AROMATHERAPY Essential oils used in vaporizers or in the bath aid relaxation and help to still the mind during meditation. For shock, nervous tension or anxiety, try a few drops of Neroli on a tissue, which you can sniff when you feel most unhappy, or try a combination of the essential oils suggested here. You can work with 10–15 drops of essential oil in a vaporizer, a maximum of 6 drops of essential oil in a full bath or 8 drops in 20 ml of a carrier oil if you are applying the essential oils for massage. If the person receiving the bath or the massage is pregnant or breastfeeding, under 12 years of age, has sensitive skin or a serious medical condition, please contact an aromatherapist before applying essential oils to the skin.

7 Change how you respond

The way we perceive and respond to a stressor is often what makes the situation harder to deal with. Your existing responses may mean that you are easily talked into doing things that you don't have the time or inclination to do. These suggestions will help you to manage your time.

ACTIVE LISTENING. These simple techniques help you to make sure that you are completely focussed on the person speaking. Check that you understand what they are saying, and ensure that they have had a chance to express themselves clearly. This kind of focussed attention helps you to avoid any misunderstandings, to build

∨ Listening skills
Focus, eye contact and relevant questions all help to create effective communication.

Pause for thought

Aim to take time out to consider any problem and your response to it before reacting. With the one exception of physical danger to yourself or others, most 'challenges' will benefit from some time to think before you tackle them. The same goes with people. If you are asked to take on a job or a responsibility that you are unsure about, ask for a little time to get back to the person with an answer, and stick to what you say.

deeper relationships or mend those in which communication is suffering. Make eye contact whilst the person is speaking. Stop what you are doing to listen to them whilst they are speaking, let them speak without interruption and only ask questions that relate to the topic under discussion and that are open-ended (so they have to answer with more than a 'yes' or 'no'). Then paraphrase what the person said to show that you have understood it properly.

THE BROKEN RECORD. Often people don't hear what you are saying to them if you are trying to say 'no' without causing offence. The broken record technique requires you to find an inoffensive sentence that makes it clear that you are unable to do what they ask. You repeat it without variation until the

> **Broken record**
This technique helps establish your boundaries, encourages others to delegate appropriately and set reasonable tasks. It can also show how and when you are able to provide support outside your remit.

< A positive spin
Using more positive language to describe things leaves you feeling more secure in your ability to cope. Negativity has the opposite effect.

< Take time
Before responding, clarify deadlines and the nature of the task. Then prioritize accordingly to avoid senseless rushing.

person you are speaking to registers what you are saying. For instance, if your boss unexpectedly wants you to stay at work very late one evening, say 'I have to leave work at 5.30 tonight'. No explanations, no excuses, simply state your boundaries.

CHANGE THE WORDS. Your body and mind believe everything you say. Using more positive words to describe your personal situation and whatever issues you are facing is effective not only in raising your self-esteem, but also in helping you to feel more confident of your success and more relaxed about the situation. Problems become 'challenges' and chaos becomes 'opportunities for change'. Focus your mind on seeking solutions rather than on restating the problem.

DON'T RUSH YOUR RESPONSE. Asking people to clarify the nature of the task, the deadlines and what their expectations are can help you both to establish shared priorities. It can also help you to maintain control over your own schedule.

8 Alter your work habits

Taking a detailed look at how you work as well as the kind of stress that work adds to your life can make a huge difference, especially if the problem lies with the amount of unpredictable or uncontrollable stress involved in your day-to-day life. Try some of the following ideas to bring a more relaxed approach to your working life:

∨ Home work
Try working at home when you need extended quiet to concentrate.

> Public transport
Whilst frequently crowded, using buses and trains lets you catch up on reading and planning your day.

> Clean desk
Tidying your workstation at the end of the day encourages a clear mind in the morning.

< Repetitive strain
Check that your workstation is appropriately organized to avoid physical discomfort at work.

CONSIDER THE JOURNEY TO WORK.
If extensive driving is making you unhappy, re-evaluate how you travel to work as well as the length of time it takes. One option may be switching to public transport and using the time gained to catch up on your reading or correspondence. Or, if possible, you could walk or cycle all or part of the way.

NEGOTIATE WORKING AT HOME. If your work requires undisturbed periods for creative thinking, working from home on a regular basis can be extremely effective.

WRITE LISTS OF THINGS TO DO. This will help you prioritize your tasks so that important things get done when they are required.

OPERATE A CLEAN DESK POLICY. No matter how busy you are, spend five minutes at the end of the day tidying your work to help put you in a more relaxed frame of mind when you arrive the following morning.

CONSIDER DOWNSHIFTING. The decision to change your career for one with either fewer financial benefits or in a less

◄ *Time out*
You can work more effectively if you take regular short breaks, avoid frequent overtime and take time off to recover when you are sick.

prestigious setting can bring about abrupt changes in your stress levels. People often downshift because of the improved quality of life that will accompany a move to a quieter area, or because a job switch will allow them more free time in which to relax.

TAKE REGULAR BREAKS. Taking five minutes every hour just to get up and stretch your legs can make a big difference. Even if deadlines are looming, a short break can help you to return to your task revitalized.

TRY TO AVOID WORKING OVERTIME.
Whilst there is often a need to stay late to finish a particular task, try not to make this a regular occurrence.

Examine your expectations

What is holding you at your place of work? Do you find your work satisfying? Are you enjoying the tasks involved? What are the most stressful elements of the job and do the satisfactory elements of your work outweigh the awkward times? Is work affecting your quality of life or the quality of time you have for your personal life?

9 Change your eating habits

Diet can be a major factor in aiding relaxation and reducing stress, especially where food allergies or intolerances exist. Eating foods to which you are mildly intolerant can cause a range of unpleasant symptoms and add to the stress load for your body. As well as dealing with emotional stress, it will also have to cope with the physical stress of fighting off foods that are not beneficial to it.

REDUCE CAFFEINE INTAKE. Whilst caffeine is an effective stimulant when you are tired, its effects include raising your blood pressure and heart rate as well as other actions that mimic the alarm stage of the stress response. Caffeine's effects are long lasting. Try and restrict your caffeine intake to a couple of cups of tea, coffee or caffeinated soft drinks per day, or less if you are having difficulties sleeping.

INCREASE YOUR WATER INTAKE. Tiredness, fatigue and lethargy can be linked to dehydration. Increasing your water intake can help to improve these symptoms, and assist in improving your skin, reducing any oedema that has developed. Oedema in the tissues often develops during stressful times so that the body can maintain the higher blood pressure and has somewhere to store toxins produced as a result of a high intake of foods you are intolerant to.

△ *Rehydrate*
Drinking two litres of water a day can flush out toxins and reduce fatigue or lethargy.

REDUCE YOUR INTAKE OF FATTY FOODS. The temptation to snack on foods high in sugar or fat during times of stress is natural; your body wants the extra energy. However, such foods increase the stress on your body.

AVOID FOODS TO WHICH YOU ARE INTOLERANT. The most common allergens are wheat, dairy, nuts and eggs. Those with strong allergies to food substances will be aware of them, yet a mild intolerance can leave you with a range of uncomfortable physical and emotional symptoms. Identify any foods that disagree with you by keeping a diary of everything you eat and drink for two weeks and comparing it with your physical and emotional state.

EAT REGULARLY. Establishing regular mealtimes will bring additional control and structure to your life and ensure that your blood-sugar levels remain constant throughout the day.

CHEMICAL STRESSORS INCLUDE

Tea	Nicotine
Coffee	Sugar (especially refined sugars)
Cola-flavoured soft drinks	
Caffeine of any description	Foods high in fat
Alcohol	Sodium (salt)

Vitamin supplementation

A multi-vitamin can help to ensure that you are getting all the nutrients that you need to function effectively. Vitamins that are particularly useful for those experiencing high levels of stress include B vitamin complexes, and Vitamin C and zinc to support the immune system at this difficult time.

AVOID EATING WHERE YOU WORK. The temptation to continue working whilst eating will be huge. Give yourself the short breaks you deserve.

INCREASE YOUR INTAKE OF FRESH FOOD. Whilst you may look to pre-prepared meals to save time cooking, they do not provide you with the nutrients available in fresh foods. Cooking can be a creative break from your routine. Look for recipes that require a short preparation time, and increase fruit and vegetable intake.

CUT BACK ON ALCOHOL. Although it appears to relax you, alcohol acts as a depressant to your nervous system, causes dehydration and, with extensive use, also raises blood pressure and heart rate. The current guidelines for alcohol consumption in the UK – that women should restrict their intake to 21 units per week and men to 28 units – is meant to be an upper limit. If you regularly drink that amount or more, reducing your intake is strongly advised.

◄ *Food for thought*
Homemade juices and a diet rich in fresh vegetables and fruits all help to provide essential vitamins and minerals to support a stressful lifestyle. Chocolate, unfortunately, doesn't.

10 Developing a stronger support network

The tend-and-befriend model (see page 7) for coping with stress and aiding relaxation does work and is an important area to look into. It is especially important if you feel cut off from others or that you lack support in your day-to-day life.

∨ *Play*
Life should not be a series of burdens. Learn from the children around you: make play a priority.

> *Help friends*
A shared activity, such as learning how to massage, can strengthen your network, provide a creative outlet and relieve stress all at the same time.

> *Social life*
Spend time with friends whose company you enjoy and with whom you can have fun.

Help with home life

If you or someone you know is having difficulties at home, social services may be able to help. Professional counsellors and a wide variety of complementary therapists also specialize in supporting you through stressful situations, aiding relaxation and suggesting ways of coping with stress.

IDENTIFY WHO YOU CAN TURN TO FOR HELP AND WHEN. You may have friends or family members who would be able and willing to help if you were in need. If you don't usually like to ask for help, it may be that they are unaware of your needs or that they don't actually know what they can do to help. Asking others for help is an effective way of including them in your life, making them feel wanted and useful.

LOOK AT PROFESSIONAL SUPPORT SERVICES. In the workplace this might include getting better access to administrative support, hiring a temporary assistant to get you through a difficult period or speaking to the human resources department if things are particularly difficult and you feel isolated from your colleagues.

CUT OUT THE DEAD WOOD. You may already be aware that some of the people you regularly associate with are not relaxing to be around. Whilst you may feel strong ties to them that you are not able or willing to give up, it may be necessary for you to limit contact with them for a while. This does not mean you should avoid seeing them ever again! Nor do you need a confrontation; simply become less available, fit contact with them into a specific task or activity that only goes on for a finite time. If you are aware that people turn to you for support above and beyond what you are currently able to provide, struggling to meet their needs can leave you feeling resentful and may not actually be serving them effectively either.

ENHANCE YOUR RELATIONSHIPS. Create good bonds with those who are able and willing to offer support. This must be a two-way relationship to be effective and of mutual benefit. Make sure that you are able to return that support in ways that they will appreciate and that make them feel cared for too. For instance, if childcare is a shared issue, offer to look after their children for the day so that they too can have time to relax.

< *Ask for help*
Identify friends or family members to whom you can really talk. Don't be afraid of asking others to help.

Index